MUSEUM OF ANTHROPOLOGY, THE UNIVERSITY OF MICHIGAN

TECHNICAL REPORTS
Number 1

CONTRIBUTIONS IN COMPUTER APPLICATIONS TO ARCHAEOLOGY
Contribution 1

A COMPUTER PROGRAM FOR
MONOTHETIC SUBDIVISIVE CLASSIFICATION IN ARCHAEOLOGY

BY

ROBERT WHALLON, JR.

ANN ARBOR
1971

© 1971 by the Regents of the University of Michigan
The Museum of Anthropology
All rights reserved

ISBN (print): 978-1-949098-48-8
ISBN (ebook): 978-1-951538-46-0

Browse all of our books at sites.lsa.umich.edu/archaeology-books.

Order our books from the University of Michigan Press at www.press.umich.edu.

For permissions, questions, or manuscript queries, contact Museum publications by email at umma-pubs@umich.edu or visit the Museum website at lsa.umich.edu/ummaa.

A COMPUTER PROGRAM FOR
MONOTHETIC SUBDIVISIVE CLASSIFICATION IN ARCHAEOLOGY

ACKNOWLEDGEMENTS

All of the computer time and services necessary for the development and testing of this program was provided me by the College of Literature, Science and the Arts. Without this generous provision of computing facilities, the development of the program would not have been possible.

I would like to thank also Roy Coppman and Les McCaughlin for their help in writing a large part of the first version of this program.

INTRODUCTION:

This report contains a brief description, operating instruction, and a source listing of a computer program for monothetic subdivisive classification in archaeology. This program was written at the University of Michigan Museum of Anthropology and is in current use there.

The method of monothetic subdivisive classification was developed in the field of plant ecology (Williams and Lambert, 1959, 1960; Lance and Williams, 1965). Recent research has shown that this approach to classification is of considerable value and interest in archaeology (Whallon, n.d.). It has been extensively applied in problems of pottery typology and also in the analysis of burials and the classification of functional areas within archaeological sites. In all of these areas, monothetic subdivision appears to offer some considerable advantages over other methods of numerical taxonomy, the most common of which are agglomerative and polythetic.

METHODS OF NUMERICAL CLASSIFICATION:

Monothetic methods of classification use only a single attribute to determine membership of an item in one or another subgroup of a typology. Polythetic methods take all attributes at once and use an index of similarity or distance based on this simultaneous consideration of all attributes. Classifications may be developed either by agglomeration, grouping individuals into larger and larger groups until all individuals are included in a single group, or by subdivision, dividing the population into smaller and smaller subgroups until the classification is considered complete by some criterion.

Monothetic agglomerative methods are obviously trivial. Classification is always completed in extremely few steps. Polythetic subdivisive methods are computationally very complex and exceedingly time-consuming. This leaves polythetic agglomerative and monothetic subdivisive approaches as the two practicable methods of numerical classification. A more complete discussion of these methods may be found in Williams and Dale (1965).

Polythetic agglomerative methods of classification have recently begun to be applied to archaeological data (Hodson, Sneath and Doran, 1966; Hodson, 1969). These methods have been widely hailed as a solution to the problem of finding an objective and replicable method for typology in archaeology (e.g. Clarke 1968:512-47). Such methods would supposedly eliminate subjective classification and replace the earlier, imperfect statistical approaches to typology (e.g. Spaulding 1953, 1960; Sackett, 1966).

Numerical taxonomy of the polythetic agglomerative sort has had some success in the analysis of archaeological data; in some instances, certainly more so than the earlier statistical methods. In other instances, however, it has not been so successful, and there are some practical problems in its general application.

NUMERICAL CLASSIFICATION IN ARCHAEOLOGY:

The logical bases for the application of various statistical methods of classification were therefore examined in the course of working with Late Woodland ceramics from New York state. Our aim was to find a statistical approach which would come close to reduplicating the traditional typology of these materials. Seriation of assemblages in which the pottery had been classified in this traditional manner had proved to be a reliable way of disclosing temporal, and to a lesser extent areal, relations between sites. This must be remembered in evaluating the following considerations. It is entirely possible that for other sorts of data or for typologies intended to reveal other kinds of variability these considerations may not be relevant. I think, however, that they are probably of quite general validity and applicability. This is discussed in more detail elsewhere (Whallon, n.d.).

The careful examination of the logic of statistical typology and of the implicit logic of traditional typology shed light on three factors which seem to indicate that polythetic agglomerative taxonomy is not a particularly appropriate method for classifying archaeological materials. Monothetic subdivisive analysis seems in this light to be more applicable.

The first two factors are the principles of shifting criteria and of a hierarchy of importance of criteria for classification. These two principles are crucial to the creation and use of most, if not all, archaeological typologies. They are generally implicit, however, and are, in fact, incongruent with the most common explicitly stated view that types consist of recurring combinations of attributes which can be shown to have historical or spatial meaning (Krieger, 1944).

Shifting Criteria

The principle of shifting criteria states that the specific attributes, and even the general classes of attributes, which are considered relevant for type definition change from one type to the next.

At one point, a pottery type may be defined by collaring (a morphological attribute) and by decorative technique (a technological attribute). At another point, pottery types may be defined on the basis of decorative motifs (stylistic attributes). This principle implies a stepwise, sequential definition of types. This in turn requires some order in which attributes are considered in the typology.

Hierarchy of Importance

The hierarchy of importance is the order in which attributes should be considered in the process of classification. This hierarchy changes at each step in the creation or use of a typology. At any given point, a certain attribute will be the most important to consider in classifying the items at hand. Another attribute will be the next more important, and so on. These attributes may, however, be the least important, virtually irrelevant, at another point in the typology. Normally, attributes are never all of equal relevance in defining types.

It is clear that the application of these two principles requires a sequential series of decisions, determining at each step the order of importance of attributes and identifying those items exhibiting the most important attribute. This results in a hierarchical, subdivisive or "tree-type" classification (Fig. 1). The tree-like diagram is a symbolic representation of the classification, which actually consists of a set of ordered questions and rules for determining to which type a particular item belongs. Each question concerns a specific attribute or characteristic which is examined at that step. The question asked at any step is determined by the specific sequence of attribute presences and absences already observed on the item in question. Not all attributes are necessarily considered in defining a type, and the number of attributes considered varies from type to type. This "tree" form of classification is a common one, familiar to us from guides to the identification of birds, trees, flowers, etc. It is a recognized kind of logical classification (cf. Kay, 1966).

It can easily be seen that polythetic agglomerative taxonomy does not and cannot implement either of the above principles. As already mentioned, polythetic agglomerative methods utilize all attributes simultaneously and equally to form similarity coefficients between items. Criteria cannot shift, therefore, and all are treated as being of equal importance.

A certain hierarchy of attributes could perhaps be obtained by weighting. This has never been attempted with archaeological materials. There is no obvious objective method for doing this, and any method which changes the weightings at each step in creating a typology would be extremely complex. Even if weightings were established, however, this would not create a hierarchy of attributes in the sense discussed above. The heaviest weighted attribute would still not have any absolute precedence in consideration over the others. It would still be combined with all other attributes in comparing items and would only have a relatively greater influence on the level of the similarity or distance coefficients between items. No matter how the coefficients are calculated, they are used as single, summary measures of similarity among items and groups of items. Types are then defined in polythetic agglomerative

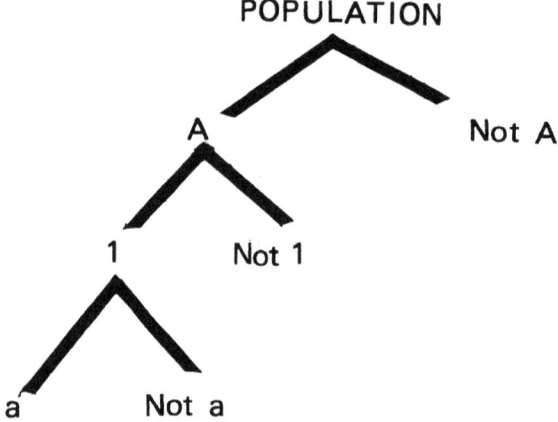

Fig. 1 A Tree-type Classification, Showing How Division Occurs In A Hierarchy. Certain Attributes Must Be Considered Before Others, And The Criteria Defining Any Type Can Be Different In Number And In The Specific Attributes Considered.

methods by clustering together items which are shown by these coefficients to be closely similar to one another. This brings us to our third consideration, that of the definability of types once a given typology has been established.

Definability of Types

The question of definability of types refers to the clarity and accuracy with which types, once defined, may be characterized or identified in terms of the original attributes utilized in their definition.

Polythetic approaches to statistical typology group items or groups of items together on the basis of similarity coefficients, which are calculated over all attributes, weighted or unweighted, exhibited by the items in the sample being analyzed. This procedure assures that those items or groups which are combined are more similar to each other, over-all, than they are to any other item or group. The specific attributes which are shared by any two items, by an item and a group, or by any two groups do not have to be the same for successive steps in the process of grouping or agglomeration. There is thus no provision nor necessity for any attribute to be possessed in common by all members of a group. Unless, however, some attribute is possessed by virtually all items in the sample, it is highly unlikely that any group of greater than trivial size will have any attributes which are common to all its members.

As a result, it is virtually impossible either to define groups or "types" established by polythetic agglomerative methods in terms of the original attributes used in the analysis. It is equally difficult to assign an item not included in the original sample and analysis to a given type by noting the attributes it exhibits. New items can eventually be assigned to one or another group only by extensive calculation of similarity coefficients, not by a simple inspection of the attributes they possess. In short, such typologies are generally abstract; and when the classified items are laid out in their respective groups, inspection does not often give the impression that these "types" are recognizable without the aid of a computer.

The above considerations may be of little importance if the types being identified are thought to have been produced involuntarily, by unconscious habits of production, and not to have been recognized within the cultural system in which they functioned. Such abstract "types" are not likely to be of great use in most current archaeological research. In the case of types which are supposed to reflect temporal and spatial variability of assemblages, the above considerations are valid and critical in the definition of types.

THE COMMON TYPOLOGICAL METHOD:

The most commonly used kind of typology in archaeology is one which is supposed to reflect temporal and spatial differences among assemblages through regularly changing proportions of the defined types. A large body of theoretical, analytical, and descriptive literature exists discussing such typologies, their formation, the cultural meaning of such types, their reality, and the techniques of seriation designed to establish the temporal or spatial relationships between assemblages once typed. Despite many differences, virtually all workers agree that these "types" must have been culturally recognized in some more or less explicit manner. This is at present the only possible way in which their regular temporal and spatial variation in proportions can be understood. The specific mechanism within a cultural system responsible for these regular fluctuations has usually been vaguely referred to as changes in "popularity" of various types.

A "type" can increase or decrease in proportionate frequency due to popularity only if every item can be quickly, easily, and definitely determined on inspection to belong to that type or not. This means, of course, that a clear definition in terms of the attributes exhibited by an item is essential. A statistical definition in terms of similarity coefficients, particularly where there is no requirement that a "type" have any attribute common to all its members, is obviously impossible.

SUMMARY OF THE PROBLEM:

We see, therefore, that archaeological typologies which have proven useful for seriation or for the study of areal distributions are defined in terms of specific attributes and attribute contributions which are distinctive and diagnostic of the various types defined. The distinctive and diagnostic attributes or combinations of attributes are not only sufficient but also necessary conditions for the assignation of any item to a given type. Furthermore, the implicit form of at least the majority of these typologies is tree-like as defined above. We find also that most recorded ethnographic classifications are tree-like (e.g. Berlin, Breedlove, and Ronen, 1968; Bulmer, 1967; Fowler and Leland, 1967; Metzger and Williams, 1966). It is possible that this form of classification is fundamental to most, if not all, uncodified typologies which are culturally recognized.

Neither the earlier numerical methods of Spaulding and Sackett nor the current methods of polythetic agglomerative classification produce objectively defined typologies which satisfy all the considerations discussed above. Monothetic subdivisive procedures, however, do produce classifications which are tree-like, follow the principles of shifting criteria and of a hierarchy of attributes, and are easily definable in terms of simple rules for observing which attributes any given item possesses. For these reasons, we have proposed them as a potentially useful approach to the problem of defining objective typologies (Whallon, n.d.).

DESCRIPTION OF PROGRAM TYPE

General

The goal of the monothetic subdivision method is to arrive at a classification in which each "type" or final group of items is uniquely defined by a specific combination of presences and absences of attributes and in which the maximum degree of homogeneity within subgroups and heterogeneity between subgroups is concurrently maintained.

At first the entire sample, and subsequently each subgroup, is subdivided on the basis of the attribute which will tend to produce the strongest differentiation between the resulting subgroups and thus the greatest internal homogeneity at that step. This means that at each subdivision as many attributes as possible will tend, as strongly as possible, to appear either in the subgroup possessing the dividing attribute or in the subgroup in which the dividing attribute is absent. The attribute which exhibits the greatest over-all tendency toward association or disassociation with other attributes is therefore the one selected as the point of subdivision at each step. The determination of which attribute shows the greatest degree of association or disassociation with the other attributes is made independently within each subgroup at each step in the development of the typology. The conditions of shifting criteria for type definition and of establishing a hierarchy of importance among attributes are thus fully satisfied. The form of the resulting typology is truly tree-like.

Although the general principles of monothetic subdivisive typology are relatively simple and require little variation from problem to problem, many of the details of implementing this method remain to be thoroughly investigated, especially when applied to archaeological materials. Some flexibility has been built into the program under discussion, therefore, permitting several details of the method used in generating a typology to be varied. These details and the options provided are discussed below. Most of these points are discussed in more detail in Whallon (n.d.).

Binary Attributes

Every attribute used in this program must be of the binary or presence/absence type. This might seem to be a disadvantage in handling archaeological data where many attributes are considered multi-state. This is not necessarily so, and the program was written specifically with such attributes in mind.

In the first place, binary attributes are much easier to program, and it is easier to define a tree-like typology with them. Beyond this, however, the use of binary attributes was derived from extensive work with

attribute associations which eventually led to the idea of applying
monothetic subdivision to archaeological data (cf. Whallon, n.d.). It
was noted that in most cases of strong association or disassociation
between multi-state attributes, almost all of the significant behavior
in the data was due to interaction between only one state of each attribute.
The interactions among the other states of each attribute showed only
random variation not indicative of any trend towards either association
or disassociation.

It was decided not to use multi-state attributes since it seemed
fruitless to divide data into several subgroups on the basis of attribute
states which exhibited no significant associations or disassociations.
Each state of a multi-state attribute was therefore redefined as an
individual binary attribute in order to allow subdivision on only that
state of an attribute which did show highly significant behavior. We
define these new attributes as members of a single attribute class and
introduce a routine for eliminating the calculation of associations or
disassociations between members of the same attribute class.

Missing Data

Missing data is accomodated by the program. An item with missing
information is omitted from any calculations for which that data is required. Certain mechanical contingencies may also call for the use of
the missing data code for accurate calculation and manipulation. If,
for example, collar decorative motifs are to be used in analysis along
with the attribute of "collaring", coding these as "missing" rather than
as absent on uncollared sherds will avoid the mechanical and unwanted high

associations between them and collaring itself.

Redundancy

An item may exhibit only one attribute from a given class of attributes as defined above. In the case of lip profiles on ceramic vessels, for example, a rim sherd can normally exhibit only a single profile. Coded as binary attributes, that one specific profile would be recorded as present on the sherd and all other profiles would be recorded as absent.

It would, of course, be nonsense to calculate the degree of association or disassociation between any two attributes of the same class. They will be totally disassociated by simple virtue of the fact of belonging to the same class. The resultant high coefficient would tell us nothing more than the fact that they belong to the same class. We therefore call testing for association between such attributes redundant and say that any attributes belonging to the same class are redundant with each other. All indexes of association between such redundant attributes can be specified and eliminated in this program.

Other pairs or sets of attributes may be related in a mechanical manner. If, for example, both plain smoothing of the surface and various decorative motifs are utilized as attributes, it is obvious that the presence of "plain surface" precludes the presence of any motif. The presence of any of the motifs, however, precludes only the attribute of plain surface. This creates a set of attributes not all of which are mutually redundant, a situation which may frequently occur with archaeological data. Such sets of redundancies can also be accomodated by the program. In this case, all exterior motifs would be specified as redundant for plain surface, but only the one attribute of plain surface would be specified for each exterior motif.

The rather complicated situation in Table 1, a set of data in which both collared and uncollared sherds occur, is an example of dealing with redundancies under this program. Collaring itself, two collar shapes, several collar decorative motifs, and several neck motifs including plain surface, are all coded as attributes. It is assumed that on both collar and neck more than one decorative motif can appear at once. In this situation we would code all the attributes as present or absent as they appear on the sherds with the exception of sherds on which there was no collar. On these sherds the collar would be coded absent but both collar shapes and all collar decorative motifs would be coded as missing data. Both collar shapes and all collar motifs would be specified as redundant for the attribute of collaring. Collaring would then be specified as redundant for each collar shape and collar decorative motif. Each of the two collar shapes would have to be specified as redundant for the other. Plain surface on the neck would be redundant for each neck motif, the neck and all neck motifs would be declared redundant with a plain surface on the neck.

Table 1

The Specification of Redundances in the Form Required for Program TYPE

Attribute	Number Of Redundancies	Redundancies				
1	5	2	3	4	5	6
2	2	1	3			
3	2	1	2			
4	1	1				
5	1	1				
6	1	1				
7	3	8	9	10		
8	1	7				
9	1	7				
10	1	7				

Note: Attributes
 1 - Collar
 2 - Collar shape a
 3 - Collar shape b
 4 - Collar motif a
 5 - Collar motif b
 6 - Collar motif c
 7 - Neck, plain surface
 8 - Neck motif a
 9 - Neck motif b
 10 - Neck motif c

The above arrangement would eliminate all meaningless comparisons between attributes of the same class and between mechanically contingent attributes. It would also prevent the inclusion of data from uncollared sherds in calculating degrees of association among attributes pertaining only to the collar and between such attributes and other attributes of the sherd. Proper manipulation of the options for specifying missing data and redundant attributes will allow the use of almost any combination of multi-state, redundant, and mechanically contingent attributes in a meaningful way.

Redundant combinations are blanked out of the printed matrix of associations and a row of asterisks appears in place of an index value.

Chi-Square Functions

The criterion for selecting the attribute on which to divide at each step is the degree of over-all association or disassociation with other attributes. In this program we have followed the original examples of monothetic subdivision from plant ecology in using the chi-square statistic to determine the degree of association between pairs of attributes. This statistic is a natural one to choose for binary or presence/absence data and can be more or less directly used as an index of association in this context where all chi-square calculations are necessarily made from fourfold tables with, in most cases, equal numbers of observations entering each table.

The various values of chi-square which are obtained for the associations of any one attribute with all other attributes must be combined in some way to provide an over-all measure of association for that attribute. The program provides three ways for doing this: using the simple sum of chi-squares, the average chi-square value, or the single largest chi-square. These various functions of chi-square are discussed in more detail in Whallon (n.d.).

The simple sum of chi-squares has been standard in monothetic subdivision in ecological applications and has proven the most satisfactory in our experiments with pottery typology. Lance and Williams (1965:247) have shown that the use of the sum of chi-squares provides a "maximum information split" in subdivision. Average chi-square is often unsatisfactory because many associations cannot be calculated in small subgroups as subdivision proceeds. This results in highly unequal numbers of individual chi-square values being used to calculate the averages for different attributes. It often happens, therefore, that an attribute with only one or two remaining calculable chi-squares will have a higher average than another attribute for which a large number of chi-squares can be calculated, even though this latter attribute may show many more individually significant chi-squares. Single largest chi-square is also not as satisfactory as sum of chi-squares because attributes with only a single, usually high value of chi-square are sometimes chosen above attributes with several moderately high and significant values. This characteristic of single largest chi-square may sometimes be desirable, however, and this option is therefore included in the program.

Other statistics such as phi have been suggested to take the place of chi-square, sometimes on the grounds that the sum of absolute values of phi will provide a "more even split" in subdivision than chi-square (Lance and Williams, 1965:247). We feel that at least some of this greater evenness is due to problems in establishing limits to the smallest expected cell frequencies accepted for the calculation of chi-square. Chi-square at least partially regains the advantage lost to phi in this way through the option of adjusting this minimum accepted expected cell value (cf. below). In certain situations, especially with sets of data in which large amounts of data are missing and the number of counts entering different chi-square tables is likely to vary considerably, the use of phi might be highly advantageous. This option is not included in the program, but it can easily be provided by the user by changing the formulas for BIN (IE, IF) in the subrountine CHISQ. The printed messages describing the output may also be modified easily to indicate that phi rather than chi-square is being used in this case.

Yates' Correction

The validity and utility of applying Yates' correction for continuity in the calculation of chi-square for this type of analysis is a debated point. The calculation of chi-square from contingency tables produces a discrete distribution of values. This is most marked in 2 x 2 tables such as those used in this program. The theoretical distribution of chi-square, to which the values obtained from contingency tables are compared for tests of significance, is a continuous distribution. The application of Yates' correction markedly improves the approximation of the discrete distribution calculated from contingency tables to the actual continuous chi-square distribution (Siegel, 1956:107). It is therefore useful and often important to apply this correction when using chi-square for testing significance of associations. From this point of view, it might also be considered desirable to apply Yates' correction in monothetic subdivision. Williams and Lambert (1959) do apply this correction. I have also customarily applied it with satisfactory results. In the few instances in which the same set of data was analyzed both with and without the application of Yates' correction, the results of the analyses were identical.

On the other hand, some workers prefer to use uncorrected values of chi-square (MacNaughton-Smith, 1965; Wishart, 1969). Their arguments may or may not be found compelling. Users of this program may wish to compare analyses carried out both with and without this correction. Because of differences of opinion regarding the value of this correction, the option to calculate the chi-square values either with or without the application of Yates' correction for continuity has been incorporated into the program.

Small Cell Values

There is a limit to how small the expected cell frequencies of a contingency table may be allowed to become if the chi-square statistic calculated from the table is to be used as a test of significance of association. This limit has been thoroughly investigated by Cochran (1952). His rules for 2 x 2 tables are that no expected cell value should be less than 5 if N is between 20 and 40, and that chi-square should not be calculated from tables with N less than 20. These rules are generally accepted as standard. They are, however, usually too rigorous for use with monothetic subdivision. Too many chi-squares are eliminated by them from analysis. It has been found in practice that it is better to relax Cochran's rules and then use chi-square only as an index of association. We thus forego any use of chi-square as a test of significance.

The lower limit to acceptable expected cell frequencies does influence the results of analysis. The question of an appropriate limit in monothetic subdivision is discussed in more detail elsewhere (Whallon, n.d.). In our experience, it has been found that a lower limit of 3 is perfectly acceptable and much more useful than 5 for typological analysis of Woodland ceramics. Even lowering the limit to .5 does not significantly alter the results of analysis. An infinitely low limit, on the other hand, in which chi-square is calculated from all tables in which no marginal total is 0, does significantly affect the results. Allowing all tables in which no marginal total is 0 to be used in analysis strikingly changes the form of the subdivision tree. In most cases with some higher limit to the smallest acceptable expected cell frequency, the splits subdividing the branches are relatively even in terms of the numbers of items falling into both subgroups at each step. When there is effectively no lower limit to smallest expected cell frequency, numerous trivial subdivisions are made, splitting single items, or occasionally pairs of items, off from the main group.

Applications of monothetic subdivision in ecology have apparently allowed the calculation and use of chi-square from all tables with expected cell frequencies greater than 0, if one can judge from the operation of Clustan I, the most general and powerful program available in this area (Wishart, 1969). It is perhaps partly for this reason that the ecologists have had some trouble with uneven splits in the process of subdivision and have suggested using other statistics such as phi in an effort to obtain more even splits (cf. above). It now appears that at least some of this problem can be overcome by setting a higher limit for minimum expected cell frequencies.

What this lower limit should optimally be is still a matter for research. It is possible that it will vary, depending upon the nature of the data being analyzed. The lower limit for acceptable expected cell frequencies has therefore been left variable in this program. It may be set from any infinitely small value (coded 0 on the control card) as used in ecological work, to as high as desired, in increments of .1.

Blank And Negative Chi-Squares

Even if any table with an infinitely small expected cell value is to be accepted, there will be some tables in which one or another column or row is blank; in other words, with one or more marginal totals of 0. It is obviously impossible and meaningless to calculate chi-square for these tables, and they are excluded from the analysis. Chi-squares for such tables are represented in the printed matrix by a row of asterisks.

Ordinarily, chi-square has no sign. A given value of chi-square represents a given degree of association or disassocation between two attributes, and only an inspection of the contingency table, in conjunction with a table of expected values, allows determination of which is the case. In this program, as a matter of convenience in the interpretation of the analysis and of the final results, chi-square values representing an association between two attributes are presented normally as positive values, while those values representing a disassociation between attributes are presented with a negative sign prefixed to them. This, of course, does not have any real statistical significance and is only an indication of the direction of association in the various tables.

Stopping Rules

One of the problems with monothetic subdivision which has received some attention in the literature is when to stop the process of subdivision. Various rules have been proposed, some practical, some attempting to establish a statistically meaningful point of termination. There are three such "stopping rules" built into this program: the number of subdividing steps made, the size of the subsets of data being analyzed, and the largest value of chi-square exhibited by the attribute on which subdivision is to be made.

At each subdivision step, all existing subgroups are considered for division. Potentially, therefore, all subgroups are available for subdivision, and the possible proliferation of subgroups is enormous, progressing as a power of 2. This program allows a maximum of 15 subdivision steps. This number naturally must be less if there are less than 15 attributes, but the potential number of resulting subgroups is, with 15 or more attributes, 2^{15}. This is an enormous and probably unmanageable and uninterpretable number of subgroups. In practice, it is highly unlikely that the actual number of subgroups will aprroach anything like 2^{15}. The number of subgroups produced is normally limited by the action of the other stopping rules. If these other rules are not applied, however, the possibility does exist of restricting the number of subgroups by limiting the number of subdivision steps made by the program.

It will normally be reasonable and desirable to implement the other stopping rules which act upon characteristics of each subgroup individually, rather than to limit the number of steps made. The first rule is that of minimal subgroup size. It is possible to specify that no subgroup smaller than a certain minimum size be further divided. This minimum size will often be determined by theoretical or practical grounds related to the nature of the material being analyzed or to the possibility of interpreting small subgroups. The size of a subgroup is also related to the statistical basis of the program. N, the total number of counts entering a fourfold table, will generally be the same as the total number of items in the subgroup being considered. Given that a certain minimum value of acceptable expected cell frequencies has been specified, it follows that there is a certain minimum size of subgroup on which analysis can be based. For any subgroup smaller than this minimum size, all fourfold tables must exhibit at least one cell value below the minimum accepted. This minimum subgroup size will obviously be four times the value of the minimum accepted expected cell frequency.

It is anticipated that there will frequently be no external reasons to limit the size of subgroups to be defined by monothetic subdivision. If this is the case, and no minimum size is specified, the program automatically determines a minimum. This minimum will be the larger of 4 or four times the minimum acceptable expected cell frequency. It should be remembered that subgroups smaller than this minimum can and will be formed, but all subgroups of this size or smaller will be set aside and will not be considered for further subdivision.

The most desirable sort of stopping rule is one related to the degree of association exhibited by the attribute on which subdivision is to occur. The basic logic of the monothetic subdivisive approach demands that subdivision on an attribute bring about some partition of items which is significant in the sense that more than one attribute shows a tendency to concentrate in one or the other of the two resultant subgroups. Some measure of the strength of association shown by the attribute on which subdivision occurs is thus probably the best criterion for stopping the process of subdivision at a given point.

A limit on the size of the sum of chi-square is not particularly useful, since the number of chi-square values included in the sum varies considerably and the values of chi-square will tend generally to decrease as N decreases. It was therefore decided to use a minimum value for the single largest chi-square exhibited by the subdividing attribute. If no non-redundant chi-square exhibited by the subdividing attribute equals or exceeds this minimum value, subdivision is terminated for that subgroup. This limit may be set by the program user at any value desired. If not specified, the value of 3.84 is automatically used by the program. This is the value for the 5 percent level of significance of association in fourfold tables.

This value has been adopted as a convenient index of association. One is tempted, in this context, to assign a statistical meaning to this value and to treat it as though it actually did represent an association stronger than would be expected by chance more than one time in twenty. It must be remembered, however, that in most cases this cannot be legitimately done. The rules limiting the acceptable size of expected cell frequencies is the use of chi-square for tests of significance will have been relaxed as discussed above. Only in those cases where the smallest acceptable expected cell value has been set at 5 will any value of chi-square be usable as a true test of significance of association. A minimum chi-square value will have to be accepted as merely an index or indicator in other instances. Still, it is the most convenient and generally the most meaningful manner in which to decide where to stop the process of subdivision.

Forcing The First Division

One of the problems often encountered in monothetic subdivision is that there will be several attributes with closely similar sums of chi-square in the original data set. The first subdivision of the data is, of course, usually made on the attribute with the highest sum. With two or more attributes showing high and similar sums, however, this procedure may not always be satisfactory. Sampling error may influence which of these closely similar sums is actually the largest in any individual sample of data. When the choice is close between two or more items, this possibility is always present.

The first split of the data is often crucial in determining the final form of the classification. Since this is the case, and since sampling error may affect the first division of the data, the possibility of forcing the first division of the data to be made on any desired attribute has been provided in the program. Decisions as to when and on what variable to force a first division must naturally be made on the basis of some prior knowledge of the materials at hand. The situation described and the desirability of forcing division on a specific attribute very rarely occurs after the first division. The possibility for forcing division is therefore limited to only the first step in analysis.

Division On A Subset Of Attributes

Provision is also made in the program for limiting the choice of attributes upon which subdivision may occur to a subset of the original number of attributes. This provision, like certain others, is specifically oriented towards the analysis of archaeological data, such as ceramics. It allows the user to specify a selected set of attributes which the program will then use for subdividing the data. All attributes are still used in analysis, and sums or averages of chi-square are calculated as as before. When the highest sum, average, or individual chi-square is sought, however, it will be sought only among the selected subset of attributes.

This option was developed with particular reference to problems of Late Woodland pottery typology. In dealing with these ceramics, it was occasionally desirable to include all attributes and all associations between attributes in the analysis and yet restrict actual subdivision to attributes of the vessel exterior (cf. Whallon, n.d.). Subdivision on attributes of the lip or interior decoration was often difficult to visualize as a basis for typology of this material. Associations between exterior attributes and lip or interior attributes were strong and significant, however, often forming a relatively large proportion of the overall strength of association of various exterior attributes. It was felt, therefore, that it would be desirable to be able to make use of all attributes and all associations in the data but to then restrict selection of attributes for subdivision to a specific subset of attributes. It remains to be seen from actual practice whether or not this option will have a significant application in archaeological analysis, but it is included and may be tried and tested.

OPERATING INSTRUCTIONS FOR PROGRAM TYPE

General

The deck arrangement for running this program with all available options is shown in Fig. 2. It will be noted that the ATTRIBUTE SELECTION CARD and REDUNDANT ATTRIBUTE CARDS are optional and will not necessarily be used for all problems.

It is assumed that the Fortran IV SOURCE DECK has been properly compiled by the user's computing facility and the resulting OBJECT DECK punched out on cards. The deck arrangement and operating instructions are presented under the assumption that this OBJECT DECK will be used when running the program with data.

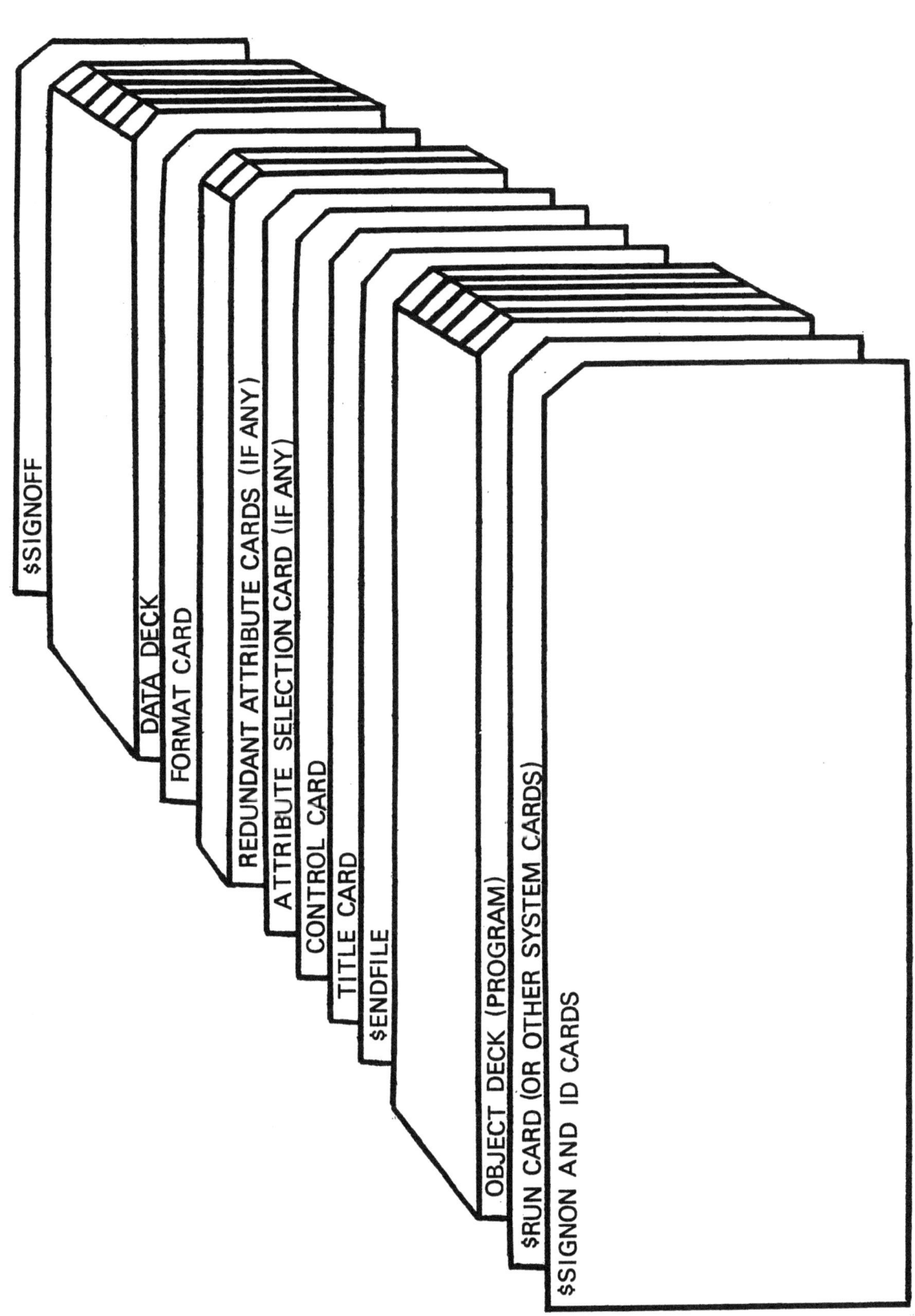

Fig. 2 Deck Set-up for Running Program TYPE

The deck arrangement is presented as it is used at the University of Michigan Computing Center, where it is processed by an IBM 360/67 computer operating under MTS (Michigan Terminal System) control. Local differences in computing facilities and especially in the operating system by which these facilities are controlled will affect the system control cards used in this deck arrangement. The form, number, and perhaps order of the following cards will perhaps be affected:

$SIGNON and ID card(s)

$RUN card

$ENDFILE card

$SIGNOFF card

Three input/output device reference numbers are used by this program, I/O units 4, 5, and 6. Control information is read in from unit 4. The data are read in from unit 5. Output is written on unit 6. The use of units 5 and 6 for input and output respectively is standard. Input on unit 4 is also standard under MTS, but may not be for other systems.

The above arrangement allows the data to be stored in a file or on tape and to be read in from their storage location separately while control information is supplied via cards through the card reader. Other systems in which I/O unit reference numbers are rigidly fixed may require modification of the above system of referencing. This can easily be done by rewriting the various READ and WRITE statements to conform to local system conventions.

Fortran IV operating under MTS allows the use of an expanded range of carriage control characters in the FORMAT statements referenced by WRITE commands. This program has, in general, been written with only standard carriage control characters in FORMAT statements, but in subroutine PRINT a carriage control character of '2' is used. Under MTS this means skip to the next half-page. On other systems which do not recognize this character, however, it has caused unpredictable problems in printing the output. If '2' is not recognized as a carriage control character, this FORMAT statement should be rewritten with a carriage control character of '1', a skip to the next page, replacing the '2'.

Running time has not been established in detail. Two examples will give an idea of its order of magnitude. A run with 15 attributes and 100 observations used 45 seconds CPU time; while 40 attributes and 89 observations required 59 seconds. One might estimate roughly a minute for a small job, ranging up to 2 or 3 minutes for larger jobs which approach the limits of the program's capacity.

Depending on the number of subdividing steps taken and on the number of attributes in the analysis, output tends to be more or less voluminous. Ample page estimates (100 or more pages) should be made until it is known approximately how many pages one's particular data will require for output. Changing the carriage control character in subroutine PRINT to '1' will significantly increase the number of pages of output.

The user should either be familiar enough with his local computing facility to assure comformity of these system control cards to the requirements of the system, or he should consult a programmer who can make whatever changes might be necessary.

Program Control Cards

The following control cards are necessary in addition to the OBJECT DECK.

<u>Title Card</u> This must be the first card read by the program. It provides a title for the printed output of up to 80 characters. Any characters legally recognized by the local system may be included in the title.

   Cols. 1 - 80   Any desired title for the output.

<u>Control Card</u> This card provides most of the information needed by the program and specifies what options are to be in effect on that particular run. All control information must be right-justified in the fields provided for it. No decimals should be punched expect in setting SMLCEL and ALCLIM and there only if desired.

   Cols. 1 - 4 ICLONG - the number of attributes in the problem. The maximum number is 40.

   Cols. 5 - 8 IRLONG - the number of objects or observations in the problem. The maximum number is 1000.

   Cols. 9 - 12 NSET - the number of attributes which are redundant with one or more other attributes. If NSET is greater than 0, REDUNDANT ATTRIBUTE CARDS must be provided. The number of REDUNDANT ATTRIBUTE CARDS must be the same as specified by NSET, i.e. one card for each redundant attribute.

   Cols. 13 - 16 ISVAR - the number of selected attributes on which division is to be allowed by the program. If this number is not specified, i.e. if ISVAR is set to 0, all attributes will be free to be chosen as dividing attributes. If a subset of selected attributes is to be specified, the number of attributes in that subset is punched in columns 13 - 16. The members of this subset must then be specified on an ATTRIBUTE SELECTION CARD included in the deck.

   Cols. 17 - 20 IHALT - the number of subdivision steps through which the program goes before terminating execution. If left 0, this number will be set to the maximum possible given the number of attributes in the particular problem and the limits of program storage.

Cols. 21 - 24 JSUM - if 0, simple sums of all non-redundant chi-squares will be used in analysis. If set to 1, the average non-redundant chi-square will be calculated and used.

Cols. 25 - 28 IFORCE - the attribute on which the first division of the data is to be forced, if desired. If left at zero, the first division will be determined in the same manner as all subsequent divisions.

Cols. 29 - 31 SMLCEL - the minimum acceptable expected cell value for the calculation of chi-square. Expressed to one decimal place -- although the decimal point need not be punched. E.g., a value of 3.0 is indicated by punching a 3 in column 30. A 0 in column 31 is optional. A value of .5 is indicated simply by punching 5 in column 31. Leaving SMLCEL blank or setting it to 0 allows any infinitely small but non-zero cell value to be accepted.

Cols. 32 - 35 ISSET - the size of subgroup at which the subgroup is put aside as too small to be considered for further divisions. Any subgroup of this size or smaller is eliminated from further analysis. If ISSET is unspecified it is set automatically by the program to a value equal to 4 x SMLCEL, or to 4 if SMLCEL is 0.

Cols. 36 - 39 KHI - if this is set to 1, the highest single chi-square value will be used as the criterion for selecting the attribute on which subdivision is to occur. (Selection between the two interacting attributes is based on which has the higher sum or average of chi-square, depending on the value of JSUM.) If KHI is left at 0, normal analysis using the sum or average of chi-squares will be carried out, depending of course on JSUM.

Cols. 40 - 43 IYATE - if 0, all chi-squares are calculated without Yates' correction for continuity; if 1, Yates' correction is applied.

Cols. 44 - 47 NODATA - the value used to indicate missing data. The default case, if this is left 0, is 9.

Cols. 48 - 52 ALCLIM - the lowest chi-square value accepted as significant. Expressed to two decimal places, though again, as for SMLCEL, the decimal point need not be punched. If the attributes selected for division by the criterion of sum of chi-squares or of average chi-square show no single chi-square equal to or greater than this value, division is terminated for that subgroup. Similarily, if the single highest chi-square is used as the criterion for division, its value must also be equal to or greater than ALCLIM or division is terminated. If ALCLIM is not specified, it is set automatically to 3.84, the 5 percent level of significance for a chi-square with one degree of freedom.

<u>Attribute Selection Card</u> If subdivision is to be allowed on only a selected subset of variables in the analysis as specified by ISVAR in columns 13 - 16 on the control card, an attribute selection card must be included in the deck. This card is omitted from the deck if ISVAR is left at 0, and division is to be allowed on any attribute. The attributes making up any selected subset are indicated on the attribute selection card in fields of two columns each, beginning with the number of the first attribute in columns 1 - 2, the second variable in columns 3 - 4, and so on. Only one attribute selection card may be included in a deck, but up to 40 selected attributes, the program limit, may be specified on this card in columns 1 - 80. There must be as many attributes listed on the variable selection card as are specified for the subset by ISVAR on the control card.

<u>Redundant Attribute Cards</u> If there are redundant attributes indicated by NSET on the control card, these redundancies must be specified on a series of redundant attribute cards. Each attribute which exhibits redundancies must be specified on a separate redundant attribute card, along with the attribute with which it is redundant. There must therefore be exactly as many redundant attribute cards in the deck as there are redundant attributes specified by NSET in columns 9 - 12 of the control card. Up to 10 attributes may be specified as redundant for any given attribute.

Each card is set up as follows:

Cols. 1 - 3 - the variable for which redundancies are to be specified.

Cols. 4 - 6 - the number of other variables with which that variable shows redundancies.

Cols. 7 - 9, 10 - 12, etc. - in fields of 3, up to col. 36 - the variables with which there are redundancies. There must be as many variables punched in this series as are specified in cols. 4 - 6.

Format Card The data format must be specified on a single card in columns 1 - 80. The format must begin with a left parenthesis and end with a right parenthesis. The data must be integer and be read in under an I-type format, usually of the form nI1, where n = the number of attributes in the problem. The specification of repetition of part of the format in the form (5X, 2 (I 1, 1X), 20 I 1), involving parentheses within the format statement, is not allowed.

Data Deck Contains the data, usually with one card per item or observation. The data must be read into the program as integer data. Presence is indicated by 1, absence is indicated by 0, and missing data is coded 9, unless specified otherwise on the control card. Decimal points should therefore be avoided either in punching the data or by use of an approximate format statement.

REFERENCES CITED

Berlin, Brent, Dennis B. Breedlove, and Peter H. Ronen

    1968 Covert Cateogories and Folk Taxonomies. American Anthropologist. Vol. 70:290-299.

Bulmer, Ralph N.H.

    1967 Why Is the Cossoway Not a Bird? A Problem of Zoological Taxonomy Among the Karam of the New Guinea Highlands. Man (n.s.) Vol. 2:5-25.

Clarke, David L.

    1968 Analytical Archaeology. Methuen & Co. London.

Cochran, W.G.

    1952 The χ^2 Test of Goodness of Fit. Annals of Mathematical Statistics. Vol. 23:315-45.

Fowler, Catherine S. and Joy Leland

    1967 Some Northern Paiute Native Categories. Ethnology. Vol. 6: 381-404.

Hodson, F.R.

    1969 Searching for Structure Within Multivariate Archaeological Data. World Archaeology. Vol. 1:90-105.

Hodson, F.R., P.H.A. Sneath, and J.E. Doran

    1966 Some Experiments in the Numerical Analysis of Archaeological Data. Biometrika. Vol. 53:311-24.

Kay, Paul

    1966 Comment. On Ethnographic Semantics: A Preliminary Survey, by B.N. Colby. Current Anthropology. Vol. 7:20-3.

Krieger, Alex D.

    1944 The Typological Concept. American Antiquity. Vol. 9:271-88.

Lance, G.N. and W.T. Williams

    1965 Computer Programs for Monothetic Classification ("Association Analysis"). Computer Journal. Vol. 8:246-9.

MacNaughton-Smith, P.

    1965 Some Statistical and Other Numerical Techniques for Classifying Individuals. Her Majesty's Stationery Office. London.

Metzger, Duane and Gerald Williams

    1966 Some Procedures and Results in the Study of Native Categories: Tzeltal Firewood. American Anthropologist. Vol. 68:389-407.

Sackett, James R.

    1966 Quantitative Analysis of Upper Paleolitic Stone Tools. In Recent Studies in Paleoanthropology, edited by J. Desmond Clark and F. Clark Howell. American Anthropologist. Vol. 68 (2.2):356-94.

Siegel, Sidney

    1956 Nonparametric Statistics for the Behavioral Sciences. McGraw-Hill Book Co. New York.

Spaulding, Albert C.

    1953 Statistical Techniques for the Discovery of Artifact Types. American Antiquity. Vol. 18:305-13.

    1960 Statistical Description and Comparison of Artifact Assemblages. In The Application of Quantitative Methods in Archaeology, edited by R.F. Heizer and S.F. Cook. Viking Fund Publications in Anthropology 28:60-83.

Whallon, Robert, Jr.

    n.d. A New Approach to Pottery Typology. American Antiquity (in press).

Williams, W.T. and M.B. Dale

    1965 Fundamental Problems in Numerical Taxonomy. In Advances in Botanical Research, edited by R.D. Preston. Academic Press. New York.

Williams, W.T. and J.M. Lambert

    1959 Multivariate Methods in Plant Ecology I. Association Analysis in Plant Communities. Journal of Ecology. Vol. 47:83-107.

    1960 Multivariate Methods in Plant Ecology II. The Use of an Electronic Digital Computer for Association Analysis. Journal of Ecology. Vol. 48:698-710.

Wishart, David

    1969 Clustan I. University of St. Andrews, Computing Laboratory. St. Andrews, Fife, Scotland.

Source Listing:

```
FORTRAN IV G COMPILER        MAIN           07-19-71        22:20.56        PAGE 0001

0001            DIMENSION HD(20),FMT(20),SUM(40)
0002            INTEGER*2 IARAY,IRNUM(1000),ICNUM(40),IHEAD(56),NSELT(40),MSET(40)
               1,NOT(40)
0003            COMMON /DATMAT/IARAY(1000,56)/CHIMAT/BBIN(40,40)
0004            READ(4,101)HD
0005            READ(4,100)ICLONG,IRLONG,NSET,ISVAR,IHALT,JSUM,IFORCE,SMLCEL,ISSET
               1,KHI,IYATE,NODATA,ALCLIM
0006        100 FORMAT(7I4,F3.1,4I4,F5.2)
0007            IF (ISVAR.GT.0) READ(4,98) (NSELT(I),I=1,ISVAR)
0008         98 FORMAT(40I2)
0009            IF(NSET.GT.0)CALL REDUN(NSET)
0010            READ(4,101)FMT
0011        101 FORMAT(20A4)
0012            IF(IHALT.EQ.0.AND.ISVAR.EQ.0)IHALT=ICLONG
0013            IF(IHALT.EQ.0.AND.ISVAR.GT.0)IHALT=ISVAR
0014            IF(IHALT.GT.15)IHALT=15
0015            IF(ISSET.EQ.0.AND.SMLCEL.GE.1.)ISSET=SMLCEL*4.+.5
0016            IF(SMLCEL.EQ.0..AND.ISSET.EQ.0)ISSET=4
0017            IF(NODATA.EQ.0)NODATA=9
0018            IF(ALCLIM.EQ.0.)ALCLIM=3.84
0019            WRITE(6,116)HD
0020            WRITE(6,96)IRLONG
0021         96 FORMAT('0SAMPLE SIZE=',I4)
0022            IF(ISVAR.EQ.0)GO TO 150
0023            WRITE(6,151)
0024        151 FORMAT('0DIVISION WILL BE ALLOWED ONLY ON THE FOLLOWING SELECTED V
               1ARIABLES:')
0025            WRITE(6,106)(NSELT(I),I=1,ISVAR)
0026        150 IF(NSET.GT.0)CALL REDWRT
0027            WRITE(6,91)ISSET
0028         91 FORMAT('0THE MINIMUM SIZE SUBGROUP ON WHICH DIVISION MAY OCCUR IS:
               1',I3)
0029            WRITE(6,89)IHALT
0030         89 FORMAT('0THE MAXIMUM NUMBER OF STEPS ALLOWED IS:',I3)
0031        155 WRITE(6,97)SMLCEL
0032         97 FORMAT('0THE SMALLEST EXPECTED CELL VALUE ACCEPTED FOR THE CALCULA
               1TION OF CHI SQUARE IS:',F4.1)
0033            WRITE(6,94)ALCLIM
0034         94 FORMAT('0THE SMALLEST ACCEPTED SIGNIFICANT CHI SQUARE IS:',F8.2)
0035            IF(IYATE.EQ.0)WRITE(6,93)
0036         93 FORMAT('0CHI SQUARES CALCULATED WITHOUT YATES CORRECTION!')
0037            IF(IYATE.NE.0)WRITE(6,95)
0038         95 FORMAT('0ALL CHI SQUARES CALCULATED WITH YATES CORRECTION')
0039            CALL INIL
0040            DO 1 N=1,ICLONG
0041          1 ICNUM(N)=N
0042            DO 2 N=1,IRLONG
0043          2 IRNUM(N)=N
0044            READ(5,FMT)((IARAY(JX,JY),JY=1,ICLONG),JX=1,IRLONG)
      C
      C         FIRST DIVISION OF THE DATA
      C
0045            CALL CHISQ(IRLONG,IRNUM,ICNUM,ICLONG,SMLCEL,IYATE,NSET)
0046            CALL ADD(SUM,ICLONG,JSUM)
0047            WRITE(6,116)HD
```

```
FORTRAN IV G COMPILER        MAIN           07-19-71        22:20.56        PAGE 0002

0048              WRITE(6,118)
0049          118 FORMAT('0ALL ORIGINAL DATA')
0050              CALL PRENT(ICNUM,ICLONG,SUM,JSUM)
0051              LEVEL=1
0052              LTEMP=2
0053              IF(IFORCE-0)5,5,4
0054            4 INFO=IFORCE
0055              WRITE(6,102)
0056          102 FORMAT('0 THE LEVEL *** 1 *** DATA SET DIVISION HAS BEEN FORCED')
0057              GO TO 8
0058            5 IF(NSET.EQ.0.OR.KHI.EQ.1.OR.JSUM.EQ.0)GO TO 131
0059              CALL BIG(SUM,ICLONG,INFO,ISVAR,NSELT)
0060              WRITE(6,119)LEVEL
0061          119 FORMAT('0A LEVEL ***',I3,' *** DATA SET DIVISION HAS BEEN MADE ON
                 1THE HIGHEST AVERAGE NON-REDUNDANT CHI SQUARE')
0062              GO TO 8
0063          131 IF(KHI-1)7,6,7
0064            6 CALL BIGCHI(SUM,ICLONG,INFO,VAL,ISVAR,NSELT,&132,&133)
0065          132 WRITE(6,103)LEVEL
0066          103 FORMAT('0 A LEVEL ***',I3,' *** DATA SET DIVISION HAS BEEN MADE ON
                 1 THE HIGHEST SINGLE NON-REDUNDANT CHI SQUARE')
0067              GO TO 8
0068          133 WRITE(6,123)
0069          123 FORMAT('0NO DIVISION. NO SIGNIFICANT CHI SQUARES OR NO VALID VARIA
                 1BLES REMAINING')
0070              GO TO 23
0071            7 CALL BIG(SUM,ICLONG,INFO,ISVAR,NSELT)
0072              WRITE(6,104)LEVEL
0073          104 FORMAT('0 A LEVEL ***',I3,' *** DATA SET DIVISION HAS BEEN MADE ON
                 1 THE HIGHEST SUM OF CHI SQUARES')
0074            8 WRITE(6,105)
0075          105 FORMAT(' VARIABLES INVOLVED IN THIS DIVISION ARE:')
0076              IF(ISVAR.EQ.0)WRITE(6,106)(ICNUM(J),J=1,ICLONG)
0077              IF(ISVAR.GT.0)WRITE(6,106)(NSELT(J),J=1,ISVAR)
0078          106 FORMAT(' ',5X,40(I2,1X))
0079              WRITE(6,107)INFO
0080          107 FORMAT('0 VARIABLE ON WHICH DIVISION HAS OCCURRED IS NUMBER',I3)
0081              KI=41
0082              CALL SCREEN(KI,INFO,ICNUM,IRNUM,IRLONG,NODATA,HD)
0083              IF(LEVEL.GE.IHALT)GO TO 23
0084              IDEX=0
      C
      C
      C     LOOP FOR ALL HIGHER LEVEL DIVISIONS
      C
0085              DO 333 I=1,IRLONG
0086          333 IF(IARAY(I,56).NE.9999)IARAY(I,56)=0
0087              KCUT=0
0088         1000 DO 21 JL=1,IRLONG
0089              IST=40+LEVEL
0090              JP=JL+1
0091              IF(IARAY(JL,56).EQ.9999)GO TO 500
0092              IF(IARAY(JL,56).EQ.9998)GO TO 21
      C
      C     FOR EACH NEW INDEX ROW SEPARATES DATA INTO GROUP FOR SUBDIVISION
      C
```

```
FORTRAN IV G COMPILER        MAIN             07-19-71        22:20.56        PAGE 0003

0093              DO 9 JM=1,LEVEL
0094              JQ=40+JM
0095              IARAY(JL,56)=IARAY(JL,56)+1
0096              DO 9 JN=JP,IRLONG
0097              IF(IARAY(JN,56).EQ.9999)GO TO 9
0098              IF(IARAY(JN,56).EQ.9998)GO TO 9
0099              IF(IARAY(JN,JQ).EQ.IARAY(JL,JQ))IARAY(JN,56)=IARAY(JN,56)+1
0100            9 CONTINUE
        C
        C         SCREENS THE SUBSET CONSTRUCTED
        C         SETS UP VECTOR OF DATA SET NAMES AND COUNTS NUMBER IN SUBSET
        C
0101              JR=0
0102              DO 10 JS=1,IRLONG
0103              IF(IARAY(JS,56).NE.LEVEL)GO TO 10
0104              JR=JR+1
0105              IRNUM(JR)=JS
0106           10 CONTINUE
        C
        C         SCREENS OUT TOO SMALL DATA SUBSETS
        C
0107              IF(JR.GE.ISSET)GO TO 1111
0108              WRITE(6,116)HD
0109          116 FORMAT('1',20A4)
0110              DO 11 JT=1,JR
0111           11 IARAY(IRNUM(JT),56)=9999
0112              WRITE(6,115)(IARAY(JL,K),K=41,IST)
0113          115 FORMAT('0THE FOLLOWING DIVISION SEQUENCE DEFINES A SUBGROUP TOO SM
                 1ALL FOR FURTHER DIVISIONS:',15I3)
0114              GO TO 17
        C
        C
0115         1111 JSEL=0
0116              JV=0
0117              DO 13 JW=1,ICLONG
0118              JZ=0
0119              DO 12 JY=41,IST
0120              JEXP=IARAY(JL,JY)
0121              JWW=IABS(JEXP)
0122           12 IF(JWW.EQ.JW)JZ=JZ+1
0123              IF(JZ.NE.0)GO TO 13
0124              JV=JV+1
0125              ICNUM(JV)=JW
0126              IF(ISVAR.EQ.0)GO TO 13
0127              DO 121 I=1,ISVAR
0128              IF(JW.EQ.NSELT(I)) GO TO 122
0129          121 CONTINUE
0130              GO TO 13
0131          122 JSEL=JSEL+1
0132              MSET(JSEL)=JW
0133              NCT(JSEL)=JV
0134           13 CONTINUE
0135              CALL CHISQ(JR,IRNUM,ICNUM,JV,SMLCEL,IYATE,NSET)
0136              CALL ADD(SUM,JV,JSUM)
0137              WRITE(6,116)HD
```

```
FORTRAN IV G COMPILER        MAIN           07-19-71       22:20.56      PAGE 0004

0138              WRITE(6,117)(IARAY(JL,K),K=41,IST)
0139          117 FORMAT('0SUBGROUP DEFINED BY:',15I4/)
0140              CALL PRENT(ICNUM,JV,SUM,JSUM)
0141              IF(ISVAR.GT.0.AND.JSEL.EQ.0)GO TO 135
0142              IF(NSET.EQ.0.OR.KHI.EQ.1.OR.JSUM.EQ.0)GO TO 141
0143           14 CALL BIG(SUM,JV,INFO,JSEL,NOT)
0144              CALL CHECK(ALCLIM,INFO,JV,IACT)
0145              IF(IACT.EQ.1)GO TO 142
0146              WRITE(6,92)ICNUM(INFO),ALCLIM
0147           92 FORMAT(/'0NO DIVISION.'/'VARIABLE',I3,' WITH HIGHEST AVERAGE HAS N
                 10 CHI SQUARE GREATER THAN SET LIMIT OF',F5.2)
0148              GO TO 17
0149          142 WRITE(6,119)LTEMP
0150              GO TO 20
0151          141 IF(KHI-1)16,15,16
0152           15 CALL BIGCHI(SUM,JV,INFO,VAL,JSEL,NOT,&134,&135)
0153          134 IF(VAL.GT.ALCLIM)GO TO 18
0154              WRITE(6,108)VAL,ALCLIM
0155          108 FORMAT(/'0 NO DIVISION. HIGHEST SINGLE CHI SQUARE',F8.2,1X,'IS LES
                 1S THAN SET LIMIT OF',F8.2)
0156              GO TO 17
0157          135 WRITE(6,123)
0158              GO TO 17
0159           16 CALL BIG(SUM,JV,INFO,JSEL,NOT)
0160              CALL CHECK(ALCLIM,INFO,JV,IACT)
0161              IF(IACT.EQ.1)GO TO 19
0162              WRITE(6,109)ICNUM(INFO),ALCLIM
0163          109 FORMAT(/'0NO DIVISION.'/'VARIABLE',I3,' WITH HIGHEST SUM HAS NO CH
                 1I SQUARE GREATER THAN SET LIMIT OF',F5.2)
0164           17 DO 171 I=1,JR
0165          171 IARAY(IRNUM(I),56)=9999
0166              IDEX=IDEX+1
0167              IF(IDEX.LT.2**LEVEL)GO TO 201
0168              WRITE(6,110)
0169          110 FORMAT(///'0 NO DIVISION HAS OCCURRED WITHIN ANY DATA SUBSET. EXEC
                 1UTION TERMINATED.')
0170              GO TO 23
0171           18 WRITE(6,103)LTEMP
0172              GO TO 20
0173           19 WRITE(6,104)LTEMP
0174           20 WRITE(6,105)
0175              IF(ISVAR.EQ.0)WRITE(6,106)(ICNUM(J),J=1,JV)
0176              IF(ISVAR.GT.0)WRITE(6,106)(MSET(J),J=1,JSEL)
0177              WRITE(6,107)ICNUM(INFO)
0178              KI=41+LEVEL
0179              CALL SCREEN(KI,INFO,ICNUM,IRNUM,JR,NODATA,HD)
0180          201 DO 202 I=1,IRLONG
0181              IF((IARAY(I,56).NE.9998).AND.(IARAY(I,56).NE.9999))IARAY(I,56)=0
0182          202 CONTINUE
0183              GO TO 21
0184          500 KOUT=KOUT+1
0185              IF(KOUT-IRLONG)21,501,501
0186           21 CONTINUE
      C
      C     END OF COMPUTING LOOP FOR ONE DIVISION LEVEL.
```

```
FORTRAN IV G COMPILER        MAIN              07-19-71        22:20.56        PAGE 0005

                C
                C     RESET INDICES FOR NEXT LOOP
                C
     0187             KCUT=0
     0188             LEVEL=LEVEL+1
     0189             LTEMP=LEVEL+1
     0190             IF(LEVEL.GE.IHALT)GO TO 23
     0191             DO 22 I=1,IRLONG
     0192          22 IF(IARAY(I,56).NE.9999)IARAY(I,56)=0
     0193             IDEX=0
     0194             GO TO 1000
     0195         501 WRITE(6,114)
     0196         114 FORMAT(///'0 ALL AVAILABLE ITEMS CLASSIFIED. EXECUTION TERMINATED.
                     1')
     0197          23 WRITE(6,116)HD
     0198             WRITE(6,111)
     0199             WRITE(6,112)
     0200             WRITE(6,113)
     0201         111 FORMAT('0',5X,100(1H*))
     0202         112 FORMAT(' ',5X,100(1H*))
     0203         113 FORMAT('    DATA STORAGE AND CODING ARRAY AT DYNAMIC TERMINATION')
     0204             DO 24 I=1,55
     0205          24 IHEAD(I)=I
     0206             DO 25 I=1,IRLONG
     0207          25 IRNUM(I)=I
     0208             CALL IPRINT(IHEAD,IRNUM,IRLONG,HD)
     0209             WRITE(6,112)
     0210             WRITE(6,112)
     0211             END

TOTAL MEMORY REQUIREMENTS 00290A BYTES
```

```
FORTRAN IV G COMPILER          CHISQ           07-19-71      22:21.10        PAGE 0001

0001            SUBROUTINE CHISQ(N,ITEMS,ISTUF,NSC,SMALL,IYATES,NSET)
0002            DIMENSION CHI(8)
0003            INTEGER*2 ITEMS(1000),ISTUF(40),IRAY
0004            COMMON/DATMAT/IRAY(1000,56)/CHIMAT/BIN(40,40)
0005            DATA ZDIV/4H****/
0006            DO 1 I=1,40
0007            DO 1 J=1,40
0008          1 BIN(I,J)=0.0
0009            IF (NSET .GT. 0) CALL REDOUT (ISTUF,NSC)
0010            IC=NSC-1
0011            DO 5 IE=1,IC
0012            ID=IE+1
0013            DO 5 IF=ID,NSC
0014            IF(BIN(IE,IF).EQ.ZDIV)GO TO 5
0015            DO 2 IG=1,8
0016          2 CHI(IG)=0.0
0017            DO 3 IH=1,N
0018            IL=ISTUF(IE)
0019            IM=ISTUF(IF)
0020            IJ=ITEMS(IH)
0021            UGH=IRAY(IJ,IM)
0022            ARG=IRAY(IJ,IL)
0023            IF(ARG.EQ.1.0.AND.UGH.EQ.1.0)CHI(1)=CHI(1)+1.0
0024            IF(ARG.EQ.1.0.AND.UGH.EQ.0.0)CHI(2)=CHI(2)+1.0
0025            IF(ARG.EQ.0.0.AND.UGH.EQ.1.0)CHI(3)=CHI(3)+1.0
0026            IF(ARG.EQ.0.0.AND.UGH.EQ.0.0)CHI(4)=CHI(4)+1.0
0027          3 CONTINUE
0028            CHI(5)=CHI(1)+CHI(2)
0029            CHI(6)=CHI(3)+CHI(4)
0030            CHI(7)=CHI(1)+CHI(3)
0031            CHI(8)=CHI(2)+CHI(4)
0032            DENOM=CHI(7)*CHI(8)*CHI(5)*CHI(6)
0033            IF(DENOM.LT.1.0)GO TO 4
0034            YCHI=CHI(5)+CHI(6)
0035            VA=(CHI(5)*CHI(7))/YCHI
0036            VB=(CHI(5)*CHI(8))/YCHI
0037            VC=(CHI(6)*CHI(7))/YCHI
0038            VD=(CHI(6)*CHI(8))/YCHI
0039            IF(VA.LT.SMALL.OR.VB.LT.SMALL.OR.VC.LT.SMALL.OR.VD.LT.SMALL)GO TO
               14
0040            XCHI=CHI(1)*CHI(4)-CHI(2)*CHI(3)
0041            IF(IYATES.EQ.0)BIN(IE,IF)=(YCHI*(XCHI)**2)/DENOM
0042            IF(IYATES.NE.0)BIN(IE,IF)=(YCHI*(ABS(XCHI)-YCHI/2.0)**2)/DENOM
0043            IF(CHI(2)*CHI(3).GT.CHI(1)*CHI(4))BIN(IE,IF)=-BIN(IE,IF)
0044            BIN(IF,IE)=BIN(IE,IF)
0045            GO TO 5
0046          4 BIN(IE,IF)=ZDIV
0047            BIN(IF,IE)=ZDIV
0048          5 CONTINUE
0049            RETURN
0050            END

TOTAL MEMORY REQUIREMENTS 0007A8 BYTES
```

```
      SUBROUTINE SCREEN(ISTOP,IVAR,IVNUM,ITNUM,NROWS,NODAT,H)
      DIMENSION H(20)
      INTEGER*2 IVNUM(40),ITNUM(1000),IGR1(1000),IGR2(1000),IGRND(500),I
     1GRERR(500),JARAY
      COMMON/DATMAT/JARAY(1000,56)
      LDX1=0
      LDX2=0
      LDXND=0
      LDXERR=0
      K=IVNUM(IVAR)
      DO 9 J=1,NROWS
      ID=ITNUM(J)
      JARAY(ID,56)=9998
      IF(JARAY(ID,K)-1)4,3,4
    3 JARAY(ID,ISTOP)=K
      LDX1=LDX1+1
      IGR1(LDX1)=ID
      GO TO 9
    4 IF(JARAY(ID,K)-0)6,5,6
    5 JARAY(ID,ISTOP)=-K
      LDX2=LDX2+1
      IGR2(LDX2)=ID
      GO TO 9
    6 IF(JARAY(ID,K)-NODAT)8,7,8
    7 JARAY(ID,56)=9999
      LDXND=LDXND+1
      IGRND(LDXND)=ID
      GO TO 9
    8 JARAY(ID,56)=9999
      LDXERR=LDXERR+1
      IGRERR(LDXERR)=ID
    9 CONTINUE
      DO 11 I=1,NROWS
      IF(JARAY(ITNUM(I),ISTOP)-K)11,10,11
   10 KDEX=ITNUM(I)
      GO TO 12
   11 CONTINUE
   12 DO 14 I=1,NROWS
      IF(JARAY(ITNUM(I),ISTOP)+K)14,13,14
   13 JDEX=ITNUM(I)
      GO TO 15
   14 CONTINUE
   15 WRITE(6,99)H
   99 FORMAT('1',20A4)
      WRITE(6,100)
  100 FORMAT('0 FIRST SUBGROUP FORMED IN THIS DIVISION IS DEFINED BY THE
     1 FOLLOWING SEQUENCE OF SUBDIVISIONS:')
      WRITE(6,101)(JARAY(KDEX,J),J=41,ISTOP)
  101 FORMAT('0',20X,15I5)
      WRITE(6,102)
  102 FORMAT('0 MEMBERS OF THIS SUBGROUP ARE:'/)
      WRITE(6,103)(IGR1(J),J=1,LDX1)
  103 FORMAT(' ',20I5)
      WRITE(6,104)
  104 FORMAT(/'0 SECOND SUBGROUP FORMED IN THIS DIVISION IS DEFINED BY T
```

FORTRAN IV G COMPILER   SCREEN   07-19-71   22:21.23   PAGE 0002

```
                       1HE FOLLOWING SEQUENCE OF SUBDIVISIONS:')
0054              WRITE(6,101)(JARAY(JCEX,J),J=41,ISTOP)
0055              WRITE(6,102)
0056              WRITE(6,103)(IGR2(J),J=1,LDX2)
0057              IF(LDXND-1)17,16,16
0058           16 WRITE(6,105)
0059          105 FORMAT(/'0 ITEMS ELIMINATED BY MISSING DATA:'/)
0060              WRITE(6,103)(IGRND(J),J=1,LDXND)
0061           17 IF(LDXERR-1)19,18,18
0062           18 WRITE(6,106)
0063          106 FORMAT(/'0 ITEMS ELIMINATED BY DATA ERRORS:'/)
0064              WRITE(6,103)(IGRERR(J),J=1,LDXERR)
0065           19 RETURN
0066              END
```

TOTAL MEMORY REQUIREMENTS 0020EC BYTES

FORTRAN IV G COMPILER   IPRINT   07-19-71   22:21.28   PAGE 0001

```
0001              SUBROUTINE IPRINT(ICCL,IROW,IR,H)
0002              DIMENSION H(20)
0003              COMMON /DATMAT/IRAY(1000,56)
0004              INTEGER*2 ICOL(56),IROW(1000),IRAY
0005              IHLIM=20
0006              ILLIM=1
0007              WRITE(6,100)(ICOL(I),I=ILLIM,IHLIM)
0008          100 FORMAT('0',4X,'**',20(I4,1X))
0009              GO TO 2
0010            1 WRITE(6,99)H
0011           99 FORMAT('1',20A4)
0012              WRITE(6,101)(ICOL(I),I=ILLIM,IHLIM)
0013            2 WRITE(6,102)
0014          101 FORMAT('0',4X,'**',20(I4,1X))
0015          102 FORMAT('0',110('*'))
0016              DO 3 I=1,IR
0017            3 WRITE(6,103)IROW(I),(IRAY(I,J),J=ILLIM,IHLIM)
0018          103 FORMAT(' ',I4,1X,'*',20(I4,1X))
0019              IF(IHLIM.EQ.56)GO TO 4
0020              ILLIM=ILLIM+20
0021              IHLIM=IHLIM+20
0022              IF(IHLIM.GT.56)IHLIM=56
0023              GO TO 1
0024            4 RETURN
0025              END
```

TOTAL MEMORY REQUIREMENTS 00039E BYTES
EXECUTION TERMINATED

```
MICHIGAN TERMINAL SYSTEM FORTRAN IV G COMPILER      FVNIL           11-29-71        12:24.44        PAGE P001

    0001              SUBROUTINE FVNIL(T)
    0002              DIMENSION T(40)
    0003              DO 1 I=1,40
    0004            1 T(I)=0.
    0005              RETURN
    0006              END
    TOTAL MEMORY REQUIREMENTS 00014A BYTES
NO ERRORS IN FVNIL




MICHIGAN TERMINAL SYSTEM FORTRAN IV G COMPILER      INIL            11-29-71        12:24.47        PAGE P001

    0001              SUBROUTINE INIL
    0002              COMMON /DATMAT/IARAY(1000,56)
    0003              INTEGER*2 IARAY
    0004              DO 1 I=1,1000
    0005              DO 1 J=1,56
    0006            1 IARAY(I,J)=0
    0007              RETURN
    0008              END
    TOTAL MEMORY REQUIREMENTS 00016C BYTES
NO ERRORS IN INIL




MICHIGAN TERMINAL SYSTEM FORTRAN IV G COMPILER      ADD             11-29-71        12:24.50        PAGE P001

    0001              SUBROUTINE ADD(S,N,JS)
    0002              COMMON /CHIMAT/XMAT(40,40)
    0003              DIMENSION S(40)
    0004              DATA SKIP/4H****/
    0005              CALL FVNIL(S)
    0006              DO 2 I=1,N
    0007              COUNT=0.
    0008              DO 1 J=1,N
    0009              IF(I.EQ.J)GO TO 1
    0010              IF(XMAT(I,J).EQ.SKIP)GO TO 1
    0011              COUNT=COUNT+1.
    0012              S(I)=S(I)+ABS(XMAT(I,J))
    0013            1 CONTINUE
    0014              IF(COUNT.EQ.0..OR.JS.EQ.0) GO TO 2
    0015              S(I)=S(I)/COUNT
    0016            2 CONTINUE
    0017              RETURN
    0018              END
    TOTAL MEMORY REQUIREMENTS 000276 BYTES
NO ERRORS IN ADD
```

```
MICHIGAN TERMINAL SYSTEM FORTRAN IV G COMPILER        REDUN          12-29-71       21:37.53

0001              SUBROUTINE REDUN(N)
0002              INTEGER*2 ISET(40,12)
0003              READ(4,1)((ISET(I,J),J=1,12),I=1,N)
0004            1 FORMAT(12I3)
0005              RETURN
0006              ENTRY REDWRT
0007              WRITE(6,100)
0008          100 FORMAT('0THE FOLLOWING REDUNDANCES HAVE BEEN REMOVED IN SUMMATIONS
                 1 OF CHI SQUARE:'/)
0009              DO 2 I=1,N
0010              L=ISET(I,2)+2
0011            2 WRITE(6,101)ISET(I,1),(ISET(I,J),J=3,L)
0012          101 FORMAT(' VARIABLE',I4,' WITH VARIABLES ',40I3)
0013              RETURN
0014              ENTRY REDOUT(IX,NX)
0015              DATA R/4H****/
0016              COMMON /CHIMAT/BIN(40,40)
0017              INTEGER*2 IX(40)
0018              DO 5 I=1,NX
0019              NROW=0
0020              DO 3 J=1,N
0021              IF(IX(I).NE.ISET(J,1)) GO TO 3
0022              NROW=J
0023              GO TO 4
0024            3 CONTINUE
0025              GO TO 6
0026            4 K=ISET(NROW,2)+2
0027              DO 5 L=3,K
0028              M=ISET(NROW,L)
0029              DO 7 IN=1,NX
0030              IF(M.EQ.IX(IN))GO TO 8
0031            7 CONTINUE
0032              GO TO 5
0033            8 BIN(I,IN)=R
0034              BIN(IN,I)=R
0035            5 CONTINUE
0036            6 CONTINUE
0037              RETURN
0038              END
     TOTAL MEMORY REQUIREMENTS 000908 BYTES
NO ERRORS IN REDUN
```

```
MICHIGAN TERMINAL SYSTEM FORTRAN IV G COMPILER        CHECK          12-29-71       21:37.54

0001              SUBROUTINE CHECK(ALIM,IC,J,IA)
0002              COMMON /CHIMAT/B(40,40)
0003              DATA Z/4H****/
0004              IA=0
0005              DO 1 K=1,J
0006              IF(B(K,IC).EQ.Z)GO TO 1
0007              IF(ABS(B(K,IC)).GE.ALIM)IA=1
0008            1 CONTINUE
0009              RETURN
0010              END
     TOTAL MEMORY REQUIREMENTS 0001FC BYTES
NO ERRORS IN CHECK
```

```
FORTRAN IV G COMPILER          PRENT          07-19-71      22:21.18      PAGE 0001

0001                SUBROUTINE PRENT(I,J,S,JS)
0002                DIMENSION S(40)
0003                INTEGER*2 I(40)
0004                COMMON /CHIMAT/AIRY(40,40)
0005                IHLIM=10
0006                ILLIM=1
0007                IF(J.LT.10)IHLIM=J
0008                WRITE(6,99)(I(K),K=ILLIM,IHLIM)
0009             99 FORMAT('0',14X,10(I3,8X))
0010                GO TO 1
0011           1000 WRITE(6,100)(I(K),K=ILLIM,IHLIM)
0012            100 FORMAT('2',14X,10(I3,8X))
0013              1 WRITE(6,101)
0014            101 FORMAT('0',120('*'))
0015                DO 2 K=1,J
0016              2 WRITE(6,102)I(K),(AIRY(K,L),L=ILLIM,IHLIM)
0017            102 FORMAT(' ',I3,7X,10(F9.2,2X))
0018                IF(JS.NE.0)GO TO 4
0019              3 WRITE(6,103)(S(L),L=ILLIM,IHLIM)
0020            103 FORMAT(4H0SUM,7X,10(F9.2,2X))
0021                GO TO 5
0022              4 WRITE(6,104)(S(L),L=ILLIM,IHLIM)
0023            104 FORMAT(4H0AVE,7X,10(F9.2,2X))
0024              5 ILLIM=ILLIM+10
0025                IF(ILLIM.GT.J)GO TO 6
0026                IHLIM=IHLIM+10
0027                IF(IHLIM.GT.J)IHLIM=J
0028                GO TO 1000
0029              6 RETURN
0030                END

TOTAL MEMORY REQUIREMENTS 00046A BYTES


FORTRAN IV G COMPILER          BIG            07-19-71      22:21.19      PAGE 0001

0001                SUBROUTINE BIG(VECT,ILONG,INFO,KSEL,NSLCT)
0002                DIMENSION VECT(40)
0003                INTEGER*2 NSLCT(40)
0004                INFO=1
0005                IF(KSEL.GT.0) INFO=NSLCT(1)
0006                DO 1 I=1,ILONG
0007                IF(KSEL.EQ.0) GO TO 3
0008                JX=0
0009                DO 2 K=1,KSEL
0010              2 IF (I.EQ.NSLCT(K)) JX=1
0011                IF(JX.EQ.0) GO TO 1
0012              3 IF(VECT(INFO).GT.VECT(I))GO TO 1
0013                INFO=I
0014              1 CONTINUE
0015                RETURN
0016                END

TOTAL MEMORY REQUIREMENTS 00027E BYTES
```

```
FORTRAN IV G COMPILER        BIGCHI           07-19-71        22;21.20        PAGE 0001

0001              SUBROUTINE BIGCHI(S,ILONG,INF,V,KSEL,NSL,*,*)
0002              DIMENSION S(40)
0003              INTEGER*2 INUM(40),NSL(40)
0004              COMMON /CHIMAT/BIN(40,40)
0005              DATA Z/4H****/
0006              V=-1.0
0007              DO 4 I=1,ILONG
0008              IF(KSEL.EQ.0)GO TO 2
0009              DO 1 KL=1,KSEL
0010              IF(I.EQ.NSL(KL))GO TO 2
0011            1 CONTINUE
0012              GO TO 4
0013            2 DO 3 J=1,ILONG
0014              IF(J.EQ.I)GO TO 3
0015              IF(BIN(I,J).EQ.Z)GO TO 3
0016              V=ABS(BIN(I,J))
0017              IT1=I
0018              IT2=J
0019              GO TO 5
0020            3 CONTINUE
0021            4 CONTINUE
0022              GO TO 13
0023            5 DO 9 I=1,ILONG
0024              IF(KSEL.EQ.0)GO TO 7
0025              DO 6 KL=1,KSEL
0026              IF(I.EQ.NSL(KL))GO TO 7
0027            6 CONTINUE
0028              GO TO 9
0029            7 DO 8 J=1,ILONG
0030              IF(J.EQ.I)GO TO 8
0031              IF(BIN(I,J).EQ.Z)GO TO 8
0032              IF(ABS(BIN(I,J)).LE.V)GO TO 8
0033              V=ABS(BIN(I,J))
0034              IT1=I
0035              IT2=J
0036            8 CONTINUE
0037            9 CONTINUE
0038              INF=IT1
0039              IF(KSEL.EQ.0)GO TO 11
0040              DO 10 KL=1,KSEL
0041              IF(IT2.EQ.NSL(KL))GO TO 11
0042           10 CONTINUE
0043              GO TO 12
0044           11 IF(S(IT2).GT.S(IT1))INF=IT2
0045           12 RETURN 1
0046           13 RETURN 2
0047              END
```

TOTAL MEMORY REQUIREMENTS 0004F2 BYTES

Sample Data and Output:

```
PROGRAM TYPE TEST DATA
   10   30   10
    1    1    2
    2    1    1
    3    1    4
    4    1    3
    5    2    6    7
    6    2    5    7
    7    2    5    6
    8    2    9   10
    9    2    8   10
   10    2    8    9
(5X,10I1)
001  1        11
002  1        11
003  1  1  1
004     1  1   1
005  1  1  1 1
006    11     1 1
007  1 1       1
008    11     11
009  1 1      11
010  1 1      11
011  1 1      11
012  1 1   1 1
013  1  1 1 1
014  1  1   11
015  1  1    11
016    11    11
017     1   1 1
018    11   1  1
019    11      1
020     1   1 1
021     1  1  1
022  1 11       1
023  1 1 1   1
024     1  1  1
025     1    1 1
026  1  1   1  1
029       1 1 1
030  1  1  1   1
031  1 1 1  1
034  1 1   1 1
```

PROGRAM TYPE TEST DATA

SAMPLE SIZE= 30

THE FOLLOWING REDUNDANCES HAVE BEEN REMOVED IN SUMMATIONS OF CHI SQUARE:

```
VARIABLE   1 WITH VARIABLES    2
VARIABLE   2 WITH VARIABLES    1
VARIABLE   3 WITH VARIABLES    4
VARIABLE   4 WITH VARIABLES    3
VARIABLE   5 WITH VARIABLES    6  7
VARIABLE   6 WITH VARIABLES    5  7
VARIABLE   7 WITH VARIABLES    5  6
VARIABLE   8 WITH VARIABLES    9 10
VARIABLE   9 WITH VARIABLES    8 10
VARIABLE  10 WITH VARIABLES    8  9
```

THE MINIMUM SIZE SUBGROUP ON WHICH DIVISION MAY OCCUR IS: 4

THE MAXIMUM NUMBER OF STEPS ALLOWED IS: 10

THE SMALLEST EXPECTED CELL VALUE ACCEPTED FOR THE CALCULATION OF CHI SQUARE IS: 0.0

THE SMALLEST ACCEPTED SIGNIFICANT CHI SQUARE IS: 3.84

CHI SQUARES CALCULATED WITHOUT YATES CORRECTION

PROGRAM TYPE TEST DATA

ALL ORIGINAL DATA

	1	2	3	4	5	6	7	8	9	10
1	0.0	******	-4.47	3.33	2.55	-1.70	0.14	2.92	-6.68	0.63
2	******	0.0	3.47	-3.00	-0.67	0.12	-0.24	-0.03	0.93	-0.92
3	-4.47	3.47	0.0	******	0.02	-0.07	-0.14	-0.00	5.29	-7.97
4	3.33	-3.00	******	0.0	0.0	0.30	0.0	-0.07	-4.57	9.23
5	2.55	-0.67	0.02	0.0	0.0	******	******	0.02	-1.01	1.15
6	-1.70	0.12	-0.07	0.30	******	0.0	******	0.29	0.37	-2.31
7	0.14	-0.24	-0.14	0.0	******	******	0.0	-0.14	-0.19	1.15
8	2.92	-0.03	-0.00	-0.07	0.02	0.29	-0.14	0.0	******	******
9	-6.68	0.93	5.29	-4.57	-1.01	0.37	-0.19	******	0.0	******
10	0.63	-0.92	-7.97	9.23	1.15	-2.31	1.15	******	******	0.0
SUM	22.41	9.38	21.44	20.49	5.42	5.16	2.00	3.46	19.03	23.37

A LEVEL *** 1 *** DATA SET DIVISION HAS BEEN MADE ON THE HIGHEST SUM OF CHI SQUARES
VARIABLES INVOLVED IN THIS DIVISION ARE:
    1 2 3 4 5 6 7 8 9 10

VARIABLE ON WHICH DIVISION HAS OCCURRED IS NUMBER 10

PROGRAM TYPE TEST DATA

FIRST SUBGROUP FORMED IN THIS DIVISION IS DEFINED BY THE FOLLOWING SEQUENCE OF SUBDIVISIONS:

10

MEMBERS OF THIS SUBGROUP ARE:

4   22   26   28

SECOND SUBGROUP FORMED IN THIS DIVISION IS DEFINED BY THE FOLLOWING SEQUENCE OF SUBDIVISIONS:

-10

MEMBERS OF THIS SUBGROUP ARE:

1   2   3   5   6   7   8   9   10   11   12   13   14   15   16   17   18   19   20   21
23   24   25   27   29   30

PROGRAM TYPE TEST DATA

SUBGROUP DEFINED BY: -10

	1	2	3	4	5	6	7	8	9
1	0.0	*********	-3.91	2.73	1.86	-1.25	0.18	6.03	-6.03
2	*********	0.0	2.28	-1.86	-0.52	0.01	-0.09	-0.54	0.54
3	-3.91	2.28	0.0	*********	0.80	-1.41	0.04	-3.53	3.53
4	2.73	-1.86	*********	0.0	-0.65	2.62	-0.52	2.87	-2.87
5	1.86	-0.52	0.80	-0.65	0.0	*********	*********	0.80	-0.80
6	-1.25	0.01	-1.41	2.62	*********	0.0	*********	-0.08	0.08
7	0.18	-0.09	0.04	-0.52	*********	*********	0.0	0.04	-0.04
8	6.03	-0.54	-3.53	2.87	0.80	-0.08	0.04	0.0	*********
9	-6.03	0.54	3.53	-2.87	-0.80	0.08	-0.04	*********	0.0
SUM	22.00	5.83	15.51	14.12	5.42	5.45	0.92	13.89	13.89

A LEVEL *** 2 *** DATA SET DIVISION HAS BEEN MADE ON THE HIGHEST SUM OF CHI SQUARES
VARIABLES INVOLVED IN THIS DIVISION ARE:
1   2   3   4   5   6   7   8   9

VARIABLE ON WHICH DIVISION HAS OCCURRED IS NUMBER   1

PROGRAM TYPE TEST DATA

FIRST SUBGROUP FORMED IN THIS DIVISION IS DEFINED BY THE FOLLOWING SEQUENCE OF SUBDIVISIONS:

    -10   1

MEMBERS OF THIS SUBGROUP ARE:

  1   3   5   7   9   10   11   12   13   14   15   23   29   30

SECOND SUBGROUP FORMED IN THIS DIVISION IS DEFINED BY THE FOLLOWING SEQUENCE OF SUBDIVISIONS:

    -10 -1

MEMBERS OF THIS SUBGROUP ARE:

  2   6   8   16   17   18   19   20   21   24   25   27

- - - Several further subdivisions are here left out - - -

PROGRAM TYPE TEST DATA

****
****

DATA STORAGE AND CODING ARRAY AT DYNAMIC TERMINATION

**	1	2	3	4	5	6	7	8	9	10	11	12	13	14	15	16	17	18	19	20
1 *	1	0	0	0	0	0	1	1	0	0	0	0	0	0	0	0	0	0	0	0
2 *	0	0	1	0	0	0	1	1	0	0	0	0	0	0	0	0	0	0	0	0
3 *	1	0	0	1	0	1	0	1	0	0	0	0	0	0	0	0	0	0	0	0
4 *	0	0	0	1	0	0	1	0	0	1	0	0	0	0	0	0	0	0	0	0
5 *	1	0	0	1	0	1	0	1	0	0	0	0	0	0	0	0	0	0	0	0
6 *	0	1	1	0	0	1	0	1	0	0	0	0	0	0	0	0	0	0	0	0
7 *	1	0	1	0	0	0	0	1	0	0	0	0	0	0	0	0	0	0	0	0
8 *	0	1	1	0	0	0	1	1	0	0	0	0	0	0	0	0	0	0	0	0
9 *	1	0	1	0	0	0	1	1	0	0	0	0	0	0	0	0	0	0	0	0
10 *	1	0	1	0	0	0	1	0	0	0	0	0	0	0	0	0	0	0	0	0
11 *	1	0	1	0	0	0	1	1	0	0	0	0	0	0	0	0	0	0	0	0
12 *	1	0	1	0	0	1	0	1	0	0	0	0	0	0	0	0	0	0	0	0
13 *	1	0	0	1	0	1	0	1	0	0	0	0	0	0	0	0	0	0	0	0
14 *	1	0	0	1	0	0	1	1	0	0	0	0	0	0	0	0	0	0	0	0
15 *	1	0	0	1	0	0	1	1	0	0	0	0	0	0	0	0	0	0	0	0
16 *	0	1	1	0	0	0	1	1	0	0	0	0	0	0	0	0	0	0	0	0
17 *	0	0	1	0	0	1	0	1	0	0	0	0	0	0	0	0	0	0	0	0
18 *	0	1	1	0	0	1	0	0	1	0	0	0	0	0	0	0	0	0	0	0
19 *	0	1	1	0	0	0	0	0	1	0	0	0	0	0	0	0	0	0	0	0
20 *	0	0	1	0	0	0	1	0	1	0	0	0	0	0	0	0	0	0	0	0
21 *	0	0	1	0	0	1	0	0	1	0	0	0	0	0	0	0	0	0	0	0
22 *	1	0	0	1	1	0	0	0	0	1	0	0	0	0	0	0	0	0	0	0
23 *	1	0	1	0	1	0	0	1	0	0	0	0	0	0	0	0	0	0	0	0
24 *	0	0	1	0	0	1	0	0	1	0	0	0	0	0	0	0	0	0	0	0
25 *	0	0	1	0	0	0	1	0	1	0	0	0	0	0	0	0	0	0	0	0
26 *	1	0	0	1	0	0	1	0	0	1	0	0	0	0	0	0	0	0	0	0
27 *	0	0	0	1	0	1	0	1	0	0	0	0	0	0	0	0	0	0	0	0
28 *	1	0	0	1	0	0	1	0	0	1	0	0	0	0	0	0	0	0	0	0
29 *	1	0	1	0	1	0	0	1	0	0	0	0	0	0	0	0	0	0	0	0
30 *	1	0	1	0	0	0	1	0	1	0	0	0	0	0	0	0	0	0	0	0

--- The printing of the blank data matrix for attributes 21 - 40 is here left out. ---

PROGRAM TYPE TEST DATA

**	41	42	43	44	45	46	47	48	49	50	51	52	53	54	55	****
1 *	-10	1	0	0	0	0	0	0	0	0	0	0	0	0	0	9999
2 *	-10	-1	0	0	0	0	0	0	0	0	0	0	0	0	0	9999
3 *	-10	1	0	0	0	0	0	0	0	0	0	0	0	0	0	9999
4 *	10	0	0	0	0	0	0	0	0	0	0	0	0	0	0	9999
5 *	-10	1	0	0	0	0	0	0	0	0	0	0	0	0	0	9999
6 *	-10	-1	0	0	0	0	0	0	0	0	0	0	0	0	0	9999
7 *	-10	1	0	0	0	0	0	0	0	0	0	0	0	0	0	9999
8 *	-10	-1	0	0	0	0	0	0	0	0	0	0	0	0	0	9999
9 *	-10	1	0	0	0	0	0	0	0	0	0	0	0	0	0	9999
10 *	-10	1	0	0	0	0	0	0	0	0	0	0	0	0	0	9999
11 *	-10	1	0	0	0	0	0	0	0	0	0	0	0	0	0	9999
12 *	-10	1	0	0	0	0	0	0	0	0	0	0	0	0	0	9999
13 *	-10	1	0	0	0	0	0	0	0	0	0	0	0	0	0	9999
14 *	-10	1	0	0	0	0	0	0	0	0	0	0	0	0	0	9999
15 *	-10	1	0	0	0	0	0	0	0	0	0	0	0	0	0	9999
16 *	-10	-1	0	0	0	0	0	0	0	0	0	0	0	0	0	9999
17 *	-10	-1	0	0	0	0	0	0	0	0	0	0	0	0	0	9999
18 *	-10	-1	0	0	0	0	0	0	0	0	0	0	0	0	0	9999
19 *	-10	-1	0	0	0	0	0	0	0	0	0	0	0	0	0	9999
20 *	-10	-1	0	0	0	0	0	0	0	0	0	0	0	0	0	9999
21 *	-10	-1	0	0	0	0	0	0	0	0	0	0	0	0	0	9999
22 *	10	0	0	0	0	0	0	0	0	0	0	0	0	0	0	9999
23 *	-10	1	0	0	0	0	0	0	0	0	0	0	0	0	0	9999
24 *	-10	-1	0	0	0	0	0	0	0	0	0	0	0	0	0	9999
25 *	-10	-1	0	0	0	0	0	0	0	0	0	0	0	0	0	9999
26 *	10	0	0	0	0	0	0	0	0	0	0	0	0	0	0	9999
27 *	-10	-1	0	0	0	0	0	0	0	0	0	0	0	0	0	9999
28 *	10	0	0	0	0	0	0	0	0	0	0	0	0	0	0	9999
29 *	-10	1	0	0	0	0	0	0	0	0	0	0	0	0	0	9999
30 *	-10	1	0	0	0	0	0	0	0	0	0	0	0	0	0	9999

STOP   0
EXECUTION TERMINATED

www.ingramcontent.com/pod-product-compliance
Lightning Source LLC
Jackson TN
JSHW052242110426
100741JS00005B/29